The Great High Priest

Born on

Christmas Day

Bob Morris

ISBN: 978-1-78364-514-5

www.obt.org.uk

****

The Open Bible Trust
Fordland Mount, Upper Basildon,
Reading, RG8 8LU, UK.

The Great High Priest
Born on Christmas Day

Contents

Page

Introduction

Introduction

Just over 2,000 years ago, an angel of the Lord appeared in a dream to a man in Galilee named Joseph who had just discovered that his fiancée was pregnant. No doubt he was in shock. So the angel said to him:

> "Joseph, son of David, do not be afraid to take Mary home as your wife, because what is conceived in her is from the Holy Spirit. She will give birth to a son, and you are to give him the name Jesus, because he will save his people from their sins." (Matthew 1:20-21)

His name was to be Jesus, the Greek equivalent of the Hebrew *Yeshua* (Joshua), meaning "The LORD saves". The very name Jesus was a proclamation that this baby was destined to become the Saviour, not only for the Jews but for the entire world, and to be the Saviour He needed to be the Great High Priest of Israel.

At Christmas time we celebrate the coming of Jesus as prophet, priest and king. Different parts of the church seem more enamoured of the different roles of Christ. Liberal Christians seem happy with His priesthood and kingship but don't particularly like His prophetic denunciations of hypocrisy and his declarations of future judgement. Everybody seems happy to see Jesus as king, but many are rather disappointed with the kingship of His first coming. It didn't really seem to amount to very much. So when most of us think of Him as king, we look forward to His return when He comes in the full glory of divine kingship. Nevertheless, on that first Christmas ... He came as prophet, priest and king.

In this publication we will look at Jesus' birth as the coming of the great High Priest. When you mention Jesus' priestly office, the eyes of the Roman Catholics, Orthodox and liturgical churches, light up with anticipation. But with evangelicals, their eyes tend to glaze over. Aren't priests a thing of the past? Or part of a different denomination? And some think the whole church a kingdom of priests.

Whatever we might think, there is value in thinking about the birth of Jesus in the context of his priestly office. It will become clear that Jesus had to be born as a human in order to fulfil His priestly role. Perhaps as king, He could have ruled from the heights. As prophet He could have delivered His message from a distance, as angels often did. But to be the great High Priest, He had to become man.

The role of priests

The role of priests

From ancient times, even before Israel was born as a nation, human cultures had priests. Their role was primarily as mediators – people who stood between humans and their god. On the one hand they were to represent their god to the people, by telling the people what their god required! The priests in Israel had those functions, but also told the people what God had said, and what God's decision was in a crisis. At one point, the Lord said to Aaron:

"You and your sons (are to) teach the Israelites all the decrees the Lord has given them through Moses." (Leviticus 10:11)

In other words, the priests in Israel were teachers of the Law of Moses and represented God to the people. They were to teach Israel all the commands Moses had been given by God.

Another way they could teach God's will was through the Urim and Thummim[1]. We aren't sure exactly what form they took, but they were seen as belonging to God. They were stored in the breast piece of the high priest and could be consulted in times of crisis.

But as mediators between God and humans, they not only represented God to humans, they also represented humans to God. The priest pleaded with God for mercy to be shown to the people and offered prescribed sacrifices on their behalf to gain God's favour and forgiveness. Even apart from sacrifices, priests prayed for the people and brought their needs before Him. We could sum up the role of priests as being mediators and reconcilers between God and man. Such was the

---

[1] For more on the Urim and Thummim see such scriptures as Exodus 28:20; Leviticus 8:8; Numbers 27:21; Deuteronomy 33:8, and also chapter 6 (casting of Lots) in *The Miracles of the Apostles* by Michael Penny published by the Open Bible Trust and available as an eBook and a perfect bound paperback.

understanding of the priesthood at the time when Jesus was born.

Jesus as Priest

Jesus as Priest

Much could be said about Jesus' role as priest. It is very fully developed in the book of Hebrews[2]. But here we want to reflect on His priesthood in the light of His incarnation, and think about the connection between Christmas and the priesthood.

Why did Jesus have to be born as a baby to fulfil His role as prophet, priest and king? Could He not have come to the earth as a thundering prophet or conquering king with all His divine attributes in evidence? Why a baby? Because of His priestly role ... if nothing else. Christmas – the celebration of His incarnation, when Jesus took on human flesh – acknowledges the fact that His coming as a baby was integral to His coming as the Great High Priest, as the writer of Hebrews calls Him.

---

[2] See *The Superiority of Christ* by W M Henry which is a study of Christ in Hebrews. (Published by the Open Bible Trust.)

Starting at the beginning with the birth narrative, Luke tells us (Luke 2:21) that Mary's son was given the name Jesus at His circumcision on the eighth day, just as the angel had directed should happen before Jesus was even conceived (Luke 1:31). "Jesus" is the Greek equivalent of the Hebrew *Yeshua* (Joshua), which means "the Lord saves". Why was He to be called that? Because He was to save His people from their sins (Matthew 1:21). Whenever we read the words saved or Saviour, cross, suffering, lamb, we are dealing with Christ's priestly role. John did not even call Him by name when he introduced Him to the world. When he saw Him coming towards him, he said simply,

"Look, the Lamb of God who takes away the sin of the world." (John 1:29)

He is Jesus because He will save His people from their sins. So we celebrate the coming of this Great High Priest on Christmas Day[3]. We

_____

[3] It is doubtful if Christ was actually born on December 25th but he came as a human being, of that there is no doubt, and December 25th is the

celebrate the coming of God in human flesh because to fulfil His role as priest, He had to be like us: become a foetus like we did, be carried in the womb for nine months like we were, be born, develop and grow as a child and then become a teenager and a young person, just like all of us did. All of that was necessary to become the Great High Priest, and it all began on that first Christmas Day.

Christmas day is absolutely critical for Jesus' role as priest because a physical human body was absolutely necessary for Jesus' role as priest. This warrants further examination.

---

day the ancient church set aside to celebrate and remember his most important birth.

Jesus as Sacrifice

Jesus as Sacrifice

As we said earlier, the essential identity of a priest in the ancient world, and ever since, is a mediator or reconciler, someone who bridges the gap between God and humans. It works two ways: from God to humans and from humans to God. Historically, in Israel, that was done primarily through a system of sacrifices, where an animal's blood was shed. When Jesus came into the world, the writer of Hebrews tells us, things were to change.

> … when Christ came into the world, he said: "Sacrifice and offering you did not desire, but a body you prepared for me; with burnt offerings and sin offerings you were not pleased. Then I said, 'Here I am … I have come to do your will, O God.'" … He sets aside the first to establish the second. And by that will, we have been made holy through the sacrifice of the *body* of Jesus Christ once and for all. (Hebrews 10:5-10)

What God had wanted all along was that His Law would be in the minds and hearts of His people and that they would be made perfect forever.

> "This is the covenant I will make with them[4] after that time, says the Lord. I will put my laws in their hearts, and I will write them on their minds." Then He adds: "Their sins and lawless acts I will remember no more." And where these have been forgiven, sacrifice for sin is no longer necessary. (Hebrews 10:16-18)

The endless sacrifices under the Law could not accomplish that – they were not God's ultimate plan. Those rituals and laws were only a shadow, an audio-visual, if you will, a teaching tool, of the reality God had in mind (Hebrews 10:1). The reality God had in mind necessitated a *body* (Hebrews 10:10), and a priest who would say, "I have come to do your will, my God" (10:7). The whole system of sacrifices in the Old Covenant

---

[4] The house of Israel and the house of Judah; see Hebrews 8:8-12.

was set aside and to establish a New Covenant necessitated the *body* of Christ to become the final sacrifice, which alone could make the people of God holy, which alone could take away sins (10:10). It was that *body* that was born on Christmas Day and which became the vehicle of Christ's priestly office.

At the Last Supper Jesus said to His disciples, "This is my blood of the New Covenant which is poured out for many for the forgiveness of sins." His broken body and His shed blood were proof of His priestly role, and the pre-requisite of His ability to forgive sins. He told His disciples to remember Him through sharing bread and wine which were symbols of His sacrifice. Remember what Jesus said to the crowds earlier:

> "Very truly I tell you, unless you eat of the flesh of the Son of Man and drink His blood, you have no life in you … Whoever eats my flesh and drinks my blood remains in me and I in him." (John 6:53,56)

Of course, He was not speaking literally of cannibalism here. But He was teaching a profound truth about spirituality. What happens to bread when we eat it? What happens to wine when we drink it? We swallow them, they go into our stomachs and intestines, where they are digested into constituent elements and they become our body, our muscles, our sinew and skin. They become us. That is symbolically what happens when we believe in the Lord Jesus as our Saviour and identify with Christ in His death. He becomes part of us and we become part of Him. His physical body and the physical elements (the bread and the wine) at the Last Supper were a picture of what happens spiritually between believers and God ... all as a result of Christ exercising His priestly function.

> "Remain in me as I also remain in you. No branch can bear fruit by itself; it must remain in the vine. Neither can you bear fruit unless you remain in me." (John 15:4)

Christ's self-sacrifice of His human *body* has earned those who believe in Him the right and ability to live in Him, and He in them for all eternity.

Jesus as Mediator

Jesus as Mediator

When Jesus was born, more than sacrifices were eventually to be abolished; so, too, was the necessity of priestly mediators. All the priestly mediators in the Bible and throughout human history had faults. They themselves were sinful human beings and the blood of the sacrifices they offered could never take away sins (Hebrews 10:4). However, what the Old Testament laws and sacrifices did clearly teach was that without the shedding of blood there was no forgiveness of sins (Hebrews 9:22). What was needed, once and for all, was a perfect mediator and a perfect sacrifice. This mediator had to be sinless and therefore had to be God ... but He also had to shed His own blood and therefore be human. Paul summed it up nicely in 1 Timothy.

> There is one God and one mediator between God and human beings, Christ Jesus, Himself human. (1 Timothy 2:5 TNIV)

Referring to the high priests of Israel, Hebrews states:

> But only the high priest entered the inner room [the holy of holies, *KJV*, or most holy place], and that only once a year, and never without blood [of animals], which he offered for himself and for the sins the people had committed in ignorance. (Hebrews 9:7)

However, when referring to Jesus, the Great High Priest, we read:

> When Christ came as high priest ... he went through the greater and more perfect tabernacle that is not man-made ... He did not enter by means of the blood of goats and calves; but he entered the Most Holy Place once for all by his own blood, having obtained eternal redemption. (Hebrews 9:11-12)

The high priests of Israel took the blood of goats and calves into the most holy place of the tabernacle or temple on earth every year. However, when Jesus, the Great High Priest, ascended He took His own blood into the true Most Holy Place in heaven

So in order to be the mediator between God and humans, the Great High Priest had to be both God and man, human and divine. To be a man He had to be flesh and blood; he had to be born with a human *body*. Christ had to have a *body* prepared for Him (Hebrews 10:5). That is one of the reasons we celebrate His birth at Christmas. We needed a sacrifice and we needed a mediator. But there are other reasons as well why Jesus needed to have a human *body*.

Jesus as Sympathiser

Jesus as Sympathiser

The writer of Hebrews makes much of His priestly role as an ability to sympathise with us.

> We do not have a high priest who is unable to empathise with our weaknesses, but we have one who has been tempted in every way, just as we are – yet he did not sin. Let us approach God's throne of grace with confidence, so that we may receive mercy to help us in our time of need. (Hebrews 4:15-16)

He has been tempted in every way that we have, so He empathises with us – He understands from His own experience. He had a body like ours and He shared our humanity.

> Since the children have flesh and blood, He too shared in their humanity so that by His death He might … free those who all their

lives were held in slavery by their fear of death. For surely it is not angels He helps but Abraham's descendants. For this reason He had to be made like His brothers and sisters in every way, in order that He might become a merciful high priest in service to God, and that He might make atonement for the sins of the people. Because He himself suffered when he was tempted, He is able to help those who are being tempted. (Hebrews 2:14-18 TNIV)

Note the connection between Jesus' *body* and His High Priestly role – in two ways: It was with His *body* that He made atonement for us, but it was also His body that enables Him to experience the same temptations and weaknesses we have.

From our twenty-first century vantage point we sometimes have trouble picturing Jesus as a real human being, and not just God disguised as a human. The picture we have of Jesus in the gospels is remarkably human in His emotions and reactions. At one point He was totally exasperated and said to the crowd, including His disciples:

> "You unbelieving and perverse generation, how long shall I stay with you and put up with you." (Luke 9:41)

He got tired like we do and had to rest. He got hungry and needed food. He longed for human companionship in His darkest hour in Gethsemane. He cried at the tomb of Lazarus, and I am sure He cried as a little boy. One of my favourite scenes in the movie *The Passion* was a brief flashback Jesus had of when He was a little boy running. He tripped and fell. Mary came running and picked Him up, wiped off His knees and comforted Him. I am sure He cried as a baby when He was hungry for milk. Here is a place where we have to be careful in singing our theology. In one of the carols we sing:

> The cattle are lowing, the baby awakes,
> but little Lord Jesus **no** crying He makes.
> (*Away in a Manger*)

If so, He was not as human as Hebrews says He was. We would do better to sing, "Little Lord Jesus **some** crying He makes." Another questionable line comes in the hymn *I stand amazed in the Presence of Jesus the Nazarene:*

> For me it was in the garden He prayed,
> 'Not My will but Thine;'
> He had no tears for His own griefs,
> but sweat-drops of blood for mine.

Yet Hebrews tells us,

> During the days of Jesus' life on earth, He offered up prayers and petitions with loud cries and tears to the One who could save Him from death. (Hebrews 5:7)

Jesus cried and felt pain and sorrow just like you and I do. At times He was lonely and impatient, just like you and I are. He was made of the same flesh and blood that you and I have. That is why He can empathise with us as the High Priest and can call those who believe in him His brothers and sisters.

Jesus as Part of Space and Time

Jesus as Part of Space and Time

Many people debate whether God exists or not; no one can debate whether Jesus was a historical human being who walked this earth 2000 years ago. People like Tom Harpur may question whether Jesus really existed or not, but to do so he has to ignore the historical evidence[5]. One historian has said that there is more historical evidence for just the resurrection of Jesus Christ than there is for the fact that Julius Caesar even existed.

Why is that important? It is important to know that our faith is reasonable and is grounded in historical reality, not in some man-made myths.

---

[5] All the non-biblical evidence and manuscripts proving the existence of Jesus can be found in chapter 23 of *True or False? Comments and Queries about Christianity* by Michael Penny; published by the Open Bible Trust and available as both an eBook and perfect bound paperback.

The Apostle John made much of this in his first epistle. He began it by saying:

> That which was from the beginning, which we have heard, which we have seen with our eyes, which we have looked at and our hands have touched – this we proclaim concerning (Jesus), the Word of life. (1 John 1:1)

John is saying that the things he is about to write he has seen for himself; he has first-hand evidence for. This really happened and John was an eye-witness to it. All John's senses, of sight and touch and hearing, verified what he was writing. In fact, later in his epistle, he wrote:

> Every spirit that acknowledges that Jesus Christ has come in the flesh is from God. (1 John 4:2)

Peter also thought it was important to be an eye witness to what Jesus did. In speaking of the Transfiguration (the only time Jesus' divine glory was revealed on earth) he wrote:

We did not follow cleverly devised stories when we told you about the coming of our Lord Jesus in power, but we were eyewitnesses of His majesty. (2 Peter 1:16)

Our confidence in Jesus as the Great High Priest is grounded in historic reality and is verifiable, because Jesus Christ, Immanuel, God with us, was born as a human baby on Christmas day. This is no myth; it is historical fact.

Jesus as Intercessor

Jesus as Intercessor

The same Jesus who was born and who died for us, was resurrected and now lives. As the writer of Hebrews puts it,

> Because Jesus lives forever, He has a permanent priesthood. Therefore He is able to save completely those who come to God through Him, because He always lives to intercede for them. (Hebrews 7:24-25)

In other words, not only was He a high priest who *died* to save His people from their sins, He is now a high priest who *lives* to pray for them. How many people pray for us regularly? Can we name them? When I was a missionary overseas, I knew the names of many people who prayed for me. It's not so obvious now, but I know One who had always prayed for me without fail – Jesus Christ, the eternal high priest.

Such a high priest truly meets our need –
one who is holy, blameless, pure, set apart
from sinners, exalted above the heavens.
(Hebrews 7:26)

The earthly priestly role of Jesus' dying to save
His people from their sins is intimately connected
with His heavenly priestly role of praying for
those people.

Jesus as our hope for the future

Jesus as our hope for the future

It is interesting to note that in order to prove to the disciples that the resurrected Jesus, whom they had just met, was the historic Jesus the disciples had known, He showed them His *body*. Yes, it was somewhat different – it was what Paul called a spiritual/glorious body. He could walk through closed doors, but He still ate and drank with them. Luke records this somewhat humorous account about the time when the two, who had met Jesus on the Emmaus Road, returned to Jerusalem to report to the disciples:

> While they were still talking about this [the Emmaus Road encounter with Jesus] Jesus Himself stood among them and said to them, "Peace be with you." They were startled and frightened, thinking they saw a ghost. He said to them, "Why are you troubled and why do doubts rise in your minds? Look at my hands and my feet. It is

I myself! Touch me and see: a ghost does not have flesh and bones, as you see I have."

When He had said this He showed them His hands and His feet. And while they still did not believe it because of joy and amazement, He asked them, "Do you have anything here to eat?" They gave Him a piece of broiled fish, and He took it and ate it in their presence. (Luke 24:36-43)

There was continuity between His physical human *body* before and after death and in resurrection. And it was with that glorified human *body* that He ascended into heaven. In the middle of a conversation with His disciples:

… He was taken up before their very eyes and a cloud hid Him from their sight. (Acts 1:9)

That should be a great encouragement to us. We pay too little attention to the story of Christ's ascension, which has wonderful implications for us. Jesus is still human and He has ascended to the right hand of the Father. He is still the High Priest and empathises with us in our human shortcomings, even as He exercises His power and authority. We need no other mediator; no other priest.

The ascension gives us another hope:

> "… this same Jesus, who has been taken from you into heaven, will come back in the same way you have *seen* Him go into heaven." (Acts 1:11)

So said the two angels at His ascension. He has a *body* to be seen and John tells us:

> Now we are children of God, and what we will be has not yet been made known. But we know that when Christ appears, we shall be like Him, for we will see Him as He is. All who have this hope in Him purifies himself, just as He is pure. (1 John 3:2-3)

Listen to what Hebrews says of this hope:

We have this hope as an anchor for the soul, firm and secure. It enters the inner sanctuary behind the curtain, where our forerunner, Jesus, has entered on our behalf. He has become a high priest for ever, in the order of Melchizedek. (Hebrews 6:19-20)

Jesus as Forever Priest in the Order of Melchizedek

Jesus as Forever Priest in the Order of Melchizedek

Clearly Jesus was not a member of the tribe of Levi or a priest in the time-bound Aaronic priesthood. Rather He is the perfect permanent High Priest, in the order of Melchizedek, this mysterious person who was high priest of God Most High who lives forever (Hebrews 7:1-3). His name means, "King of Righteousness" and he was called "King of Peace".

Every Christmas time we should celebrate the coming of the Great High Priest – celebrate the birth of Him who came in a *body* to save His people from their sins and now continues to pray for them and give them a sure and certain hope for an eternal future with Him.

About the author

Bob Morris was born in Sarnia, Ontario, Canada in 1940. He was educated at Ontario Bible College and The University of Western Ontario. He became a qualified High School teacher and taught for ten years in Canada and overseas. He then became the Director of Interserve, a Christian agency recruiting Christian professionals to work among unreached people in closed countries and was living in both Cyprus and Canada. At present he enjoys retirement in Toronto.

****

For a full list of books available from
The Open Bible Trust,
please visit

www.obt.org.uk/books

Also on this subject

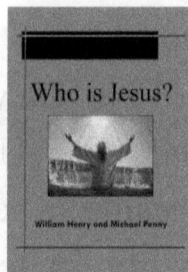

The Exceeding Great Joy of the Magi
Matthew 2
Roger Barnett

The Virgin Birth
Theo Todman)

Jesus: God and Man
Brian Sherring)

Who is Jesus?
William Henry and Michael Penny

Why in a Stable?
Roger Barnett

Further details of the books on these pages
can be seen on

www.obt.org.uk

The books are available from that website and
from

The Open Bible Trust
Fordland Mount, Upper Basildon,
Reading, RG8 8LU, UK.

They are also available as eBooks from Amazon
and Apple and as
KDP paperback from Amazon

Also by Bob Morris

Koheleth speaks!
- Ecclesiastes 3 and 4 -

The author faces the fact that Christians are now in the minority is most westernized countries, and much of the rest of the world. As such we live in a secular society with a desire for pleasure and a fear of boredom. How do Christian survive? And how do they strive for Christian values?

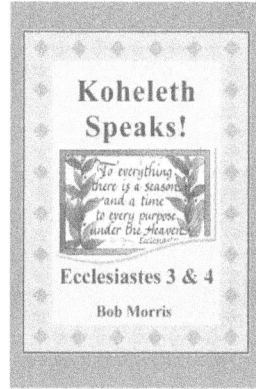

Drawing upon Ecclesiastes - "one of the most modern books in the entire Scripture" - he advocates that Christians would move society closer to Christian values if they met unbelievers where they are, and if Christians were prepared to settle for "better" solutions ... rather than going for the "best" or "nothing" scenario.

Free sample

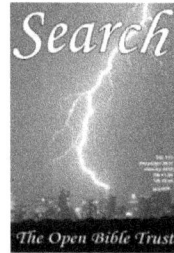

For a free sample of
the Open Bible Trust's magazine Search,
please email

admin@obt.org.uk

or visit

www.obt.org.uk/search

About this book

The Great High Priest
Born on Christmas Day

Just over 2,000 years ago, an angel of the Lord appeared in a dream to a man in Galilee named Joseph. He had just discovered that his fiancée was pregnant.

He was to learn that this Child was to be the Great High Priest in the Order of Melchizedek. As such He would be a sacrifice and a sympathiser, an intercessor and a mediator, and He was humanity's hope for the future, for eternal life.

www.ingramcontent.com/pod-product-compliance
Lightning Source LLC
Chambersburg PA
CBHW060706030426
42337CB00017B/2773

9 781783 645145